Day by day

Let's get to know Jesus
a little bit more

Jim Prestidge

WestBow Press books may be ordered through booksellers or by contacting:

WestBow Press
A Division of Thomas Nelson & Zondervan
1663 Liberty Drive
Bloomington, IN 47403
www.westbowpress.com
844-714-3454

Interior Image Credit: Mary Rose Aviles

Scripture quotations taken from the Revised English Bible, copyright © Cambridge University Press and Oxford University Press 1989. All rights reserved.

ISBN: 978-1-6642-5963-8 (sc)
ISBN: 978-1-6642-5964-5 (e)

Library of Congress Control Number: 2022903988

Print information available on the last page.

WestBow Press rev. date: 06/09/2022

WESTBOW
PRESS®
A DIVISION OF THOMAS NELSON
& ZONDERVAN

Day by day

I grow

I learn

I know Jesus a bit more

Who is God?

God is not like a person. He is good and wise. He is powerful. He is everlasting.

God created the world. He cares for the world he has made. He keeps it going. He wants it to become better. He cares for people too.

We should talk to God and get to know him. If we ask him he guides us through each day. Then our life is good and happy.

Jesus taught about God. Jesus taught us how to live. If we are good, we please God. We must trust God. Then we do not go wrong.

In the beginning God created the heavens and the earth. The earth was a vast waste, darkness covered the deep, and the spirit of God hovered over the surface of the water. God said, 'Let there be light,' and there was light; and God saw the light was good, and he separated light from darkness. He called the light day, and the darkness night. So evening came, and morning came; it was the first day.
(Genesis 1:1–5)

Prayer to begin the day

Lord
You are God.
You made everything, you keep everything going.
I honor your name.
May everyone on earth live your way.

Lord
Thank you for giving me this day.
May I walk through this day with you.

Bless my parents, sisters, brothers, my friends.
Keep us all safe.
May we all know your joy.

Lord
May we be good to each other.
May we learn new things.
May we grow as you would have us be.

This is a prayer for when you wake in the morning.
It is good to pause after each thing we have prayed.
While you pray, think about what we are saying.
Pray for anything special that will happen today.

Prayer to end the day

Lord
Thank you for this day.
Thank you for the things I have learned.
Thank you for the things I have done.
Thank you for my happiness.
Thank you for keeping me safe.

Lord
Forgive me the mistakes I have made.
Help me to do better tomorrow.
I forgive anyone who upset me.

Lord
Give me nice sleep and to wake in the morning.
Give me a good day tomorrow.
Help me to know you more.
May everyone come to know your way.

This is a prayer for bedtime.
Pray for anything that has gone wrong during the day.
Pray for your parents, sisters, brothers and friends.
Pray for your teacher to be happy and teach well.

Talking to God

We talk to God by praying.

God knows everything. He knows our thoughts. He knows what we mean to do, even if we do not quite get it right. We must always speak the truth to God. We can be silent before God, until something comes to us to say.

If we hide anything, he will know. If we admit to God that we have gone wrong, he will forget it and help us out.

Talk to God any time. We can pray while walking or riding our bicycle or on a bus. We do not have to say it out loud. He hears our thoughts.

It is good to ask God before doing anything. That checks that what we do is right.

Prayers in church

In church we say prayers from the Bible and prayers which people have written. We can use these prayers ourselves, if they are what we want to say. Sometimes they put the thing better than we can.

Always talk to God naturally, like you would talk to your teacher, or your mother or father, or your friends.

The Lord has told you mortals what is good,
and what it is that the Lord requires of you:
only to act justly, to love loyalty,
to walk humbly with your God.
(Micah 6:8)

The Lord's Prayer

Jesus told his followers, this is how you should pray.
Our Father in heaven,
may your name be hallowed;
your kingdom come,
your will be done,
on earth as in heaven.
Give us today our daily bread.
Forgive us the wrong we have done,
as we have forgiven those who have wronged us.
And do not put us to the test,
but save us from the evil one.
(Matthew 6:9–13)

In the prayer God comes first. We call him "Father". He is our heavenly father.

We pray for his name to be respected and for his Kingdom to come. Hallowed means made holy.

We come second. God already knows what we need.
Daily bread means all our food and everything else we need.
We confess things we have done wrong. We ask God to forgive us. We must forgive others as well.
We ask God to protect us.

God talks to us through the Bible. The four gospels tell the story of Jesus. Gospel means good news. In the gospels we read what Jesus taught his followers. Jesus insists that his followers do what he tells them. We must be careful to read the Bible and do as he said.

A Worthy life

Jesus told his followers to think about other people. Be considerate and helpful. Never say anything to anyone which may hurt their feelings.

Someone may be nasty to you, or say nasty things, or tell tales behind your back. Jesus said, do not fight back. Instead, be sorry for them. The fact is, they do not know nice behavior. Do not be upset. Do not avoid them. Take trouble to show them good behavior. They need to learn. Be brave. Help them become better.

God is good. Everyone has failings. We do not know our own failings. We should help each other to behave worthy of God. Ask God to show you where you fall short of his standard.

Jesus often went to a quiet place to pray, where he would not be disturbed. You can go to your bedroom, or into the garden, or a park, or a field.

Once Jesus went up a mountain to pray. On the way down he met a crowd of his followers. He stopped and taught them. It is called the Sermon on the Mount.

St Paul wrote this to the followers in Rome. He did not want them to fall into bad ways.

Conform no longer to the pattern of this present world,
but be transformed by the renewal of your minds.
Then you will be able to discern the will of God,
and to know what is good, acceptable, and perfect.
(Romans 12:2)

From the Sermon on the Mount

Blessed are those whose hearts are pure;
they shall see God.
(Matthew 5:8)

Like the lamp, you must shed light among your fellows,
so that, when they see the good you do,
they may give praise to your Father in heaven.
(Matthew 5:16)

There must be no limit to your goodness,
as your heavenly Father's goodness knows no bounds.
(Matthew 5:48)

In your prayers do not go babbling on like the heathen,
who imagine that the more they say the more likely
they are to be heard.
(Matthew 6:7)

Do not judge, and you will not be judged.
(Matthew 7:1)

Always treat others as you would like them to treat you...
(Matthew 7:12)

Always be helpful
at home, in school, when visiting.

Following Jesus

As you follow Jesus, always be truthful and honest. Be well behaved. God's people are good people. We do not harm anyone. We can always be trusted. We are always helpful.

Try to grow up to be like that. Those are the sort of people everyone likes, because they are nice. Ask God to help you. God will always show us the way.

Jesus called himself the good shepherd. A shepherd looks after a flock of sheep. Jesus looks after us. He really cares for us. We are sometimes called his flock.

A shepherd takes his flock to new pastures. In Jesus' country the shepherd went in front. He showed the sheep the way to go. He called them. They knew his voice and followed him. If we know God's voice and follow Jesus we do not go astray. He shows us what to do.

We should let God direct our life. God has a plan. He shows us how to grow up properly. He sees to it that we are all right. Following Jesus keeps us happy. He is the good shepherd. To follow Jesus is the very best thing for us.

Jesus said,
I am the good shepherd;
I know my own and my own know me.
(John 10:14)

My own sheep listen to my voice;
I know them and they follow me.
I give them eternal life and they will never perish;
no one will snatch them from my care.
(John 10:27–28)

The Good Shepherd, the Thief and the Wolf

A shepherd protects his sheep from danger. If we follow Jesus he protects us from danger. He mentioned two dangers for a flock of sheep.

There is the thief. A thief steals sheep. He takes them away.

Someone may mislead you. Some people say that there is no God. That is what they think. As you follow Jesus you get to know him. You see that God is real. In fact he is wise, good and helpful.

The other danger for sheep is the wolf. A wolf gets among the sheep. The wolf may bite them. They are frightened. They run anywhere to get away.

Jesus was thinking of Satan. Satan is another voice inside you. He puts bad ideas into your head. He suggests you tell a lie, or steal or do something else that is wrong. When you are tempted to do wrong, it is Satan tempting you.

Satan is God's enemy. He wants you to follow him, not Jesus.

Never do what Satan says. When a wrong thought comes to you, tell Satan to go away. Tell him that you listen to Jesus, not him. You can say a quick prayer silently to God. Then Satan will always leave you.

Jesus said,

'I am the good shepherd;
the good shepherd lays down his life for the sheep.
The hired man, when he sees the wolf coming,
abandons the sheep and runs away,
because he is not the shepherd and the sheep are not his.
Then the wolf harries the flock and scatters the sheep.
(John 10:11–12)

The hired man is a man paid to look after the sheep.
He does not want to get hurt by the wolf. He puts himself
first. We should never put ourselves first.

The Twenty Third Psalm

The psalms are ancient songs or poems about God. Psalm 23 is about the Lord Jesus, the good shepherd. It starts by saying that he is my shepherd, he guides me and looks after me.

The Lord is my shepherd; I lack for nothing.
He makes me lie down in green pastures,
he leads me to water where I may rest;
he revives my spirit;
for his name's sake he guides me in the right paths.
(Psalm 23:1–3)

What Psalm 23 says

By following the Lord God, we never miss out on anything we need.

The Lord God looks after us. He gives us food and rest. He gives us strength and encouragement.

The Lord God guides us through life, so that we go the right way.

Humble and helpful

It is nice when someone helps you. We should always help other people. Help anyone who is struggling. Offer to help an adult.

The opposite of being helpful is to be selfish. A selfish person thinks of themselves. Jesus always put others first.

Do not wait to be asked. Go out of your way to be helpful.

Golden rules to follow

Be humble. Let God honor you. Do not try to honor yourself.

Do not push yourself forward. It is better to be called to the front than to be told to go back.

Do not boast about what you do. Let others say it about you. Never praise yourself.

Remember the saying, 'Forgive and forget'. Swallow your hurt. Forgive them and be friends again.

Do not insist on your rights. God will sort it out best.

The Ten Commandments

The commandments are rules for behavior. They are in the Bible. The first commandments are about behavior to God. The rest are about how to behave to each other.

In those days, people were afraid of something bad happening to them. Some people made things from wood or metal and called them gods. They hoped they would protect them.

They gave their false gods food to keep them alive. Of course, they were not alive. But a stray dog came on the quiet and ate the food. Then they said their god was real, because it had eaten the food.

The first three commandments keep us faithful to God and respectful.

If we steal or tell tales then the other person feels hurt or wronged. Our relationship with them is lost.

If we kill or are unfaithful that makes a lot of trouble.

Doing wrong breaks friendships. It divides the community.

Keeping all the commandments helps us to live together happily. We can all be friends together. We can help each other and enjoy each other.

Keeping the commandments puts God in his place. It avoids squabbles. We all feel fairly treated. The commandments make for happiness.

The Commandments

1. You must have no other god besides me.
2. You must not make a carved image for yourself, nor the likeness of anything in the heavens above, or on the earth below, or in the waters under the earth.
3. You must not make wrong use of the name of the Lord your God; the Lord will not leave unpunished anyone who misuses his name.
4. Remember to keep the Sabbath day holy. You have six days to labor and do all your work; but the seventh day is a Sabbath of the Lord your God; that day you must not do any work, neither you, nor your son or your daughter, your slave or your slave-girl, your cattle, or the alien residing among you; for in six days the Lord made the heavens and the earth, the sea, and all that is in them, and on the seventh day he rested. Therefore, the Lord blessed the Sabbath day and declared it holy.
5. Honor your father and your mother, so that you may enjoy long life in the land which the Lord your God is giving you.
6. Do not commit murder.
7. Do not commit adultery.
8. Do not steal.
9. Do not give false evidence against your neighbor.
10. Do not covet your neighbor's household: you must not covet your neighbor's wife, his slave, his slave-girl, his ox, his donkey, or anything that belongs to him.

About the Commandments

God first

The first commandments tell us to look to God and honor him. The commandments begin with God. We should always put God first in everything.

The Sabbath

God gave us the Sabbath to make a break from everyday things. It is a day of rest. It gives us time to think about God and his things.

Honor your parents

We honor our parents by being respectful and polite to them. We can talk about them respectfully to our friends.

Help your parents. Offer help when they are doing something. Do not wait to be asked.

Pray for your parents. Try to make them happy.

Do not kill

If you feel very cross with someone, do not say you will kill them. Do not even say it jokingly. Do not ever think it. Life is precious. God gives birth. He is the one to end a life, not us.

Be kind to animals, not to hurt or kill them.

Adultery

Adultery is when adults are not faithful to each other.

We should be faithful to our family and to our friends.

Stealing

Your things are yours. Other people's things are theirs. Do not think of taking them.

Someone may have something you like. Do not take it from them. It is theirs. Do not envy them for having it. If you want it very much, tell God. He can help you not to have bad thoughts over it.

Telling tales

To give false evidence is to say something about somebody that is not true. Do not make up stories about anyone.

Always be honest. Never try to get anyone into trouble. Think how you would feel if they did it to you.

Coveting

Sometimes you would like something that somebody has. If you long for it, that is coveting. Coveting brings temptation.

You must resist coveting. Never long for what is someone else's. Think of things you have, and others do not have.

Friendship

Always be friendly. People take to a friendly person. God wants everybody to be friends together.

If someone is unfriendly to you, be friendly back. Show them God's way. Being friends is best.

Honor God and he will bring you good friends. A good friend is good to you. Let God choose your best friends.

In God's world, we are all friendly, kind and thoughtful. We help each other. Our behavior is good. We are humble. We are honest and true. That is the kind of person you want to grow up to be.

Do not just copy other people. If you do, you will pick up bad ways. Decide what is right and good and do it. Ask God to show you.

The best life in the world is the life God has for you. It is full of friendship and happiness.

*Put all your trust in the Lord
and do not rely on your own understanding.
At every step you take keep him in mind,
and he will direct your path.
(Proverbs 3:5–6)*

A Store of Goodness

When you visit some people, they go to their store cupboard and bring something for you. It may be a toy to play with, or something special to eat, or a present to take away.

Inside us we have a store of things that we have remembered. We can bring out memories and tell others. It is nice to have things to tell.

Day by day you build your store. There are things you have learned. There is something nice that happened. You remember a kindness. There are things you learned at school, or which someone told you. Your store is called memory.

Do not store nasty things. If someone upset you, forgive them and forget it. Ask God to help you build your store and fill it only with good things. Ask him to help you keep useless things out.

The things to remember are those which are beautiful and good. Another day you can tell your friends. You have given them something good for their store.

Your store will last all your life, so build it well. Then when you are grown up and very old you can go to it and find goodness and wisdom.

Jesus said,

*Good people from their store of good produce good;
and evil people from their store of evil produce evil.*
(Matthew 12:35)

The Vine and the Kingdom

Jesus explained God's world by giving a picture. He said that it is like a vine. A vine grows tall. Grapes grow on it. Where Jesus was, people trained vines to spread overhead. They sat in the shade under their vine when it was hot. They ate the grapes. They made wine from grapes and drank it.

In Jesus' picture, God grows the vine. He looks after it, so that it does well. Jesus is the stem. The stem supports the branches and feeds them with nutrients. We are the branches. Jesus supports and feeds us. The branches have grapes. The grapes are the things we do for God.

The parts of the vine all work together.

Jesus' picture shows us that we all work together through him. We rely on Jesus. Then our life is fruitful.

If a branch is cut off the stem then it cannot live and have grapes. It means that without Jesus we do not do as we should. With Jesus behind us, we do God's work. We are his people.

When people are supported and fed by Jesus the world works properly. That is the Kingdom of God. The Kingdom of God is not a country. It is anywhere where God rules and Jesus leads. In the Kingdom people live properly. We see bits of the Kingdom here and there. God wants his Kingdom to come everywhere.

Jesus said:

I am the vine; you are the branches.
Anyone who dwells in me, as I dwell in him, bears much fruit;
apart from me you can do nothing.
(John 15:5)

God's Way

In God's Kingdom we care for each other. We all behave well and get on together. Jesus teaches us how. Remember that Jesus is always there to show you and help you live better. You can ask God to bring you into his Kingdom.

The Kingdom of God is a way of living. It is sometimes called the Kingdom of Heaven. It is the way God made the world to work. When we live as God intended, the world works better.

We find Jesus' teaching in the Bible. Jesus said:

The time has arrived; the kingdom of God is upon you.
Repent, and believe the gospel.
(Mark 1:15)

Repent means to be sorry about something you have done wrong. When you repent, you turn away from it, never to do it again.

We should tell our friends about God's Kingdom. They should be part of it too. It is a lovely, peaceful way to live.

Jesus said that he is a light to guide us.
Those who live by the truth come to the light
so that it may be clearly seen that God is in all they do.
(John 3:21)

In God's Kingdom God's goodness fills us. It overflows.
It goes from us to others. That is a wonderful thing.

About the Author

Jim is writing this book to you. A lot of it is what he learned as a child like you. The useful things are the ones that one remembers. Jesus was the supreme teacher, the one to listen to and follow.

Jim has lived in many parts of the world. We grow up in different homes and cultures. We speak different languages. There is one language which makes us outstanding people. That is the language of God's Kingdom. It is a language about life, not words.

We do not grow out of God's language as we get older. It grows as we grow. We grow into it. We get to know Jesus a little bit more every day, even when we get very old.

Printed in the United States
by Baker & Taylor Publisher Services